.mother.

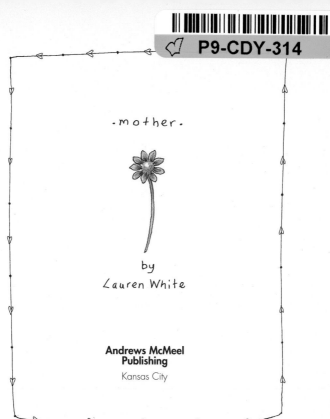

by
Lauren White

**Andrews McMeel
Publishing**

Kansas City

mother:

woman

caregiver

doctor

magician

chef

detective

organizer

therapist

accountant

coach

Surgeon · entertainer · diplomat · playmate · laundress ·

man . chauffeur . hedonist . teacher . lover . role model

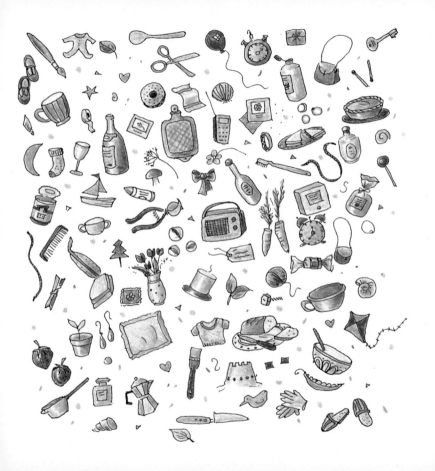

teacher

doctor

an instinct for diagnosis...

measles

broken heart

fever

nasty cough

cuts and scrapes

tummy ache

entertainer

diplomat

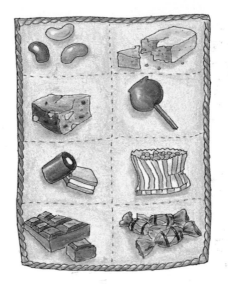

"Can I have?..."

" NO !
because
I
said
SO "

her love is unconditional

wise woman

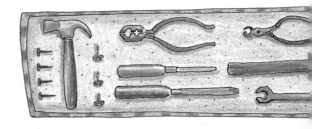

If it needs fixing, get out the tool ba
needs fixing after half an hour, put the ke

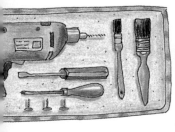

up your sleeves, and fix it, If it still
ake a cup of tea, and call someone...

· the magician's bag ·

Chameleon

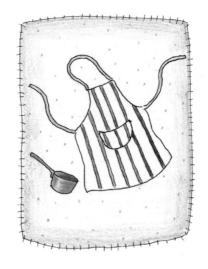

" PIT STOPS! "

organizer

TIME

WORK

PLAY

REST

MONEY

BITS + PIECES

· she uses her instincts ·

laundress

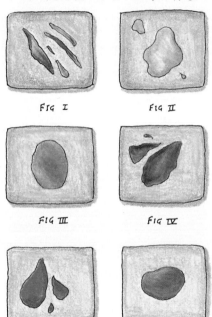

· FAVORITE STAINS ·

FIG I

FIG II

FIG III

FIG IV

FIG V

FIG VI

FIG I ~ grass

FIG II ~ egg

FIG III ~ fruit juice

FIG IV ~ mud

FIG V ~ ketchup

FIG VI ~ unknown to man

hedonist

curl up on a big cozy sofa...

pour yourself a
gin and tonic...

open the handmade
chocolates and indulge...

collector

furniture   paintings   ceramics

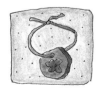 

jewelry   sculpture   fine prints

the unique and priceless treasures that come home from school...

· her time is given gladly ·

coach

smoother and soother

psychiatrist

· B L U E   M O O D S ·

an empty nest

P. m. S

never enough time

teenage angst

SLAM

feeling trapped

no light at the end of the tunnel

· the sun always rises ·

worrier

THINGS TEENAGERS DO THAT WORRY YOU

drink

smoke

drive

sulk

shop

be nice

therapist

tears

laughter

euphoria

anger

confusion

tranquillity

the emotional ups and downs...

— · she has insight · —

It can sometimes feel like si

dedly sailing on a very stormy sea...

optimist

matchmaker

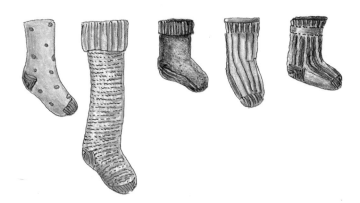

detective

not in here...

or here...

or under here...

or in here...

or here...

or down here...

found him!

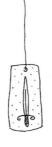

· she defends fiercely ·

a shoulder to cry on

playmate

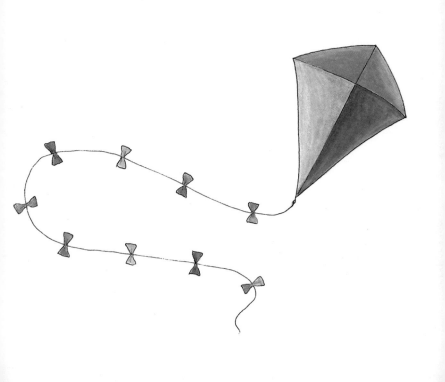

gardener

SEEDLINGS NEED...

water

food

warmth

care   attention   love

Surgeon

·solutions to leaky problems·

I. tears

II. little accidents

III. dripping faucets

I

II

III

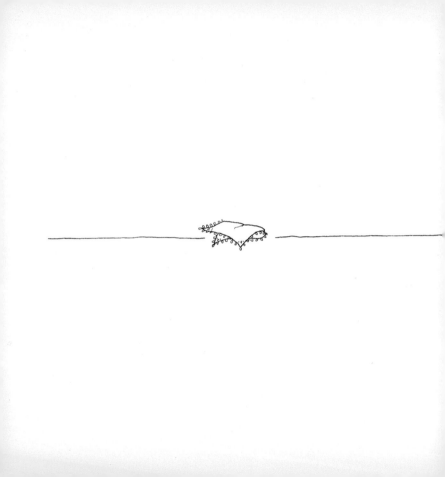

—————————— · she'll laugh with you and cry with you · ——————

chef de cuisine

voilà !

escapologist

RECLAIM THE BATHROOM!

gather together all your
favorite lotions and potions...

pour a glass of something
nice...

lie back in a warm steamy bath and
let all your cares melt away...

and wait for the little knock on the bathroom door...

temptress

pearls gorgeous perfume little black dres

dies silk stockings high heels... high hopes!

magician

balancing act

Oops!

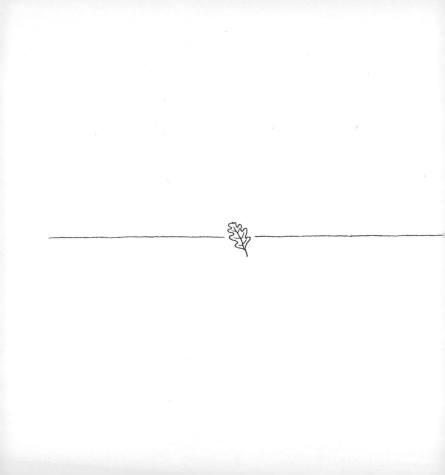

——————————— she knows what is real ———————————

Chauffeur

this   starts early...

...and just goes on and on...

sculptor

accountant

 + = FAIR SHARE

nurturer

· she acts with integrity ·

lover

bribe the baby-sitter...

chill the wine...

light the candles...

put on the soft music...

scent the air with roses...

there's all the time in the world...

until the phone rings...

role model

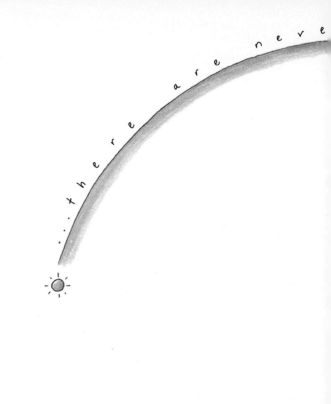

...there are neve

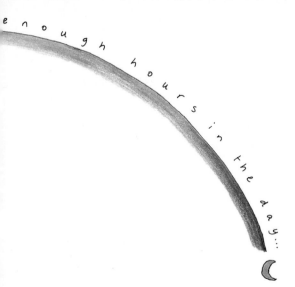

e n o u g h   h o u r s   i n   t h e   d a y...

supreme juggler

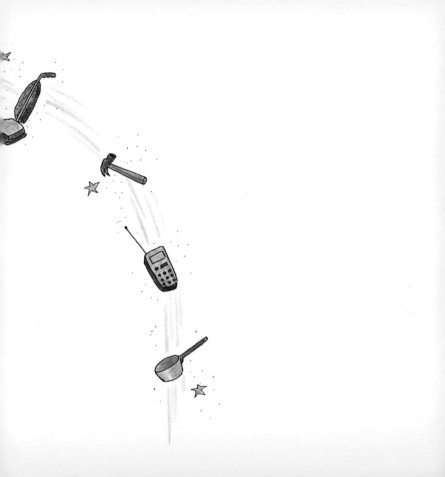

• she wants the world for you •

"Adding a sprinkling of magic to the everyday..." is how Lauren White describes her original style of drawing. Born and brought up in the village of Cranfield in Bedfordshire County, England, she studied fine art in Hull and London before returning to Bedfordshire to work as resident illustrator for a local wildlife trust. Lauren loves playing the piano, walking her dog Jack, and she carries a sketchbook everywhere she goes. She lives with her partner, Michael, and describes herself as having an astonishing collection of marbles and a wicked sense of humor. Lauren's designs for Hotchpotch greetings cards are sold around the world, and in this book she continues to refine her distinctive style which "celebrates the simple things in life."

First published by MQ Publications Limited
254–258 Goswell Road, London EC1V 7RL

Copyright © MQ Publications Limited 1999
Text & Illustrations © Lauren White 1999

ISBN: 0-8362-9275-8

Library of Congress Catalog Card Number: 98-88410

99 00 01 02 03 MQP 10 9 8 7 6 5 4 3 2 1

www.andrewsmcmeel.com

Printed and bound in Malaysia